THE SCALING

CODE

I0479796

Strategies and Techniques for Effective Management and Sustainable Company Growth

By

John Darwin

Table Of Contents

THE SCALING CODE

INTRODUCTION

Scaling people is very important in a fast growing company. In this book, we will explore the challenges and strategies of scaling people in a fast-growing organization. Scaling a company can be a thrilling experience, but it comes with its own set of challenges. As a company grows, it needs more people to keep up with demand, but the process of adding people to an organization is complex and can be difficult to manage.

People are the backbone of any organization, and scaling people is crucial to the success of a company. Hiring and developing the right talent, building a strong company culture, and developing effective leadership and management skills are all essential to scaling people. This book will explore these topics in depth, as well as communication and collaboration, scaling operations and infrastructure, and scaling culture and values.

Whether you are a founder, CEO, manager, or an employee at a scaling organization, this book is for you. We will provide practical strategies and techniques that you can use to effectively manage and scale people in your organization. In the following chapters, we will dive into the various aspects of scaling people, and provide insights and examples from successful scaling organizations. Our goal is to equip you with the tools and knowledge needed to build a sustainable and successful scaling company.

Defining scaling and its challenges

Scaling is the process of growing an organization while maintaining its quality and integrity. It involves expanding the reach, size, and operations of a business to meet the growing demand of its products or services. Scaling is an essential step for businesses to grow and become successful.

THE SCALING CODE

However, scaling also comes with its own set of challenges. One of the biggest challenges of scaling is managing the growth of the organization while maintaining quality and efficiency. As the organization expands, it becomes increasingly difficult to maintain the same level of quality and service. This can lead to a decline in customer satisfaction and brand reputation.

Another challenge of scaling is managing the complexity that comes with growth. As an organization expands, its operations become more complex and difficult to manage. This can lead to communication breakdowns, inefficient processes, and increased costs.

Furthermore, scaling also presents challenges in managing people. Hiring and retaining top talent becomes more difficult as the organization grows. Managing a larger team requires more effective leadership and management skills to ensure that everyone is aligned with the company's goals and objectives.

In summary, scaling presents both opportunities and challenges for businesses. While it can lead to increased revenue and success, it also requires effective management and planning to overcome the challenges that come with growth.

The importance of people in scaling

People are at the heart of any organization, and they are essential to the process of scaling. In fact, people are the most important asset of a scaling organization. Hiring and retaining top talent is crucial to the success of the company, and effective management of people is necessary to achieve sustainable growth.

Here are some reasons why people are important in scaling:

- People drive innovation: In a scaling organization, innovation is key to staying ahead of the competition. The people within the organization are the ones who come up with new ideas and drive innovation.

- People create the culture: A strong company culture is essential to the success of a scaling organization. The people within the organization are the ones who create and maintain the culture. A positive and supportive culture can attract and retain top talent, and help the organization to achieve its goals.
- People execute the strategy: A great strategy is only as good as its execution. The people within the organization are the ones who execute the strategy and make it a reality. Effective management of people is necessary to ensure that everyone is aligned with the strategy and working towards the same goals.
- People are the face of the company: The people within the organization are the ones who interact with customers, partners, and other stakeholders. They are the face of the company and can have a

significant impact on the company's reputation and success.

In summary, people are critical to the success of a scaling organization. Effective management and development of people can help an organization to attract and retain top talent, drive innovation, maintain a strong culture, execute the strategy, and enhance the company's reputation.

Chapter 1:Hiring and Building a Strong Team

Building a company culture that attracts top talent

Building a company culture that attracts top talent is essential to the success of a scaling organization. A strong culture can help to attract and retain top talent, improve employee engagement and productivity, and enhance the company's reputation.

Here are some strategies for building a company culture that attracts top talent:

- Define your values: A strong culture is built on a foundation of shared values. Define your company's values and make sure they are aligned with the company's mission and goals.

- Lead by example: Culture starts at the top. Leaders ought to act in the manner that they would like to see from their employees. This includes being transparent, open to feedback, and inclusive.
- Foster a sense of community: Create opportunities for employees to connect with each other and build relationships. This can include team-building activities, social events, and volunteer opportunities.
- Provide opportunities for growth and development: Top talent wants to work for an organization that values their growth and development. Provide opportunities for learning and development, including mentorship programs, training opportunities, and career advancement opportunities.
- Emphasize work-life balance: Top talent wants to work for an organization that values their well-being. Emphasize work-life balance by offering flexible schedules,

remote work options, and wellness programs.

- Celebrate successes: Celebrate the successes of your employees and the organization as a whole. This can include recognition programs, employee awards, and company-wide celebrations.

In summary, building a company culture that attracts top talent requires defining your values, leading by example, fostering a sense of community, providing opportunities for growth and development, emphasizing work-life balance, and celebrating successes. A strong culture can help to attract and retain top talent, improve employee engagement and productivity, and enhance the company's reputation.

Developing an effective hiring process

Developing an effective hiring process is critical to scaling an organization. Hiring the right people is essential to achieving sustainable growth and building a strong company culture.

Here are some strategies for developing an effective hiring process:

- Define the job requirements: Before posting a job opening, define the job requirements and the skills, experience, and qualifications necessary for the role. This will help to attract the right candidates and ensure that the job description accurately reflects the position.
- Create a diverse candidate pool: A diverse candidate pool can bring new perspectives and ideas to the organization. Develop strategies for attracting candidates from diverse backgrounds, including posting job openings on diverse job boards and attending job fairs focused on underrepresented groups.
- Use behavioral-based interview questions: Behavioral-based interview questions can help to assess a candidate's skills, experience, and personality. Develop a list of questions that are specific to the job

requirements and focus on past experiences and behaviors.

- Conduct skills assessments: Skills assessments can help to evaluate a candidate's technical skills and experience. Develop skills assessments that are specific to the job requirements and require candidates to demonstrate their skills.
- Conduct reference checks: Reference checks can provide valuable insights into a candidate's work history and performance. Develop a list of questions to ask references and verify the information provided by the candidate.
- Provide a positive candidate experience: The hiring process can impact a candidate's perception of the organization. Provide a positive candidate experience by communicating clearly, providing timely feedback, and treating candidates with respect.

In summary, developing an effective hiring process requires defining job requirements, creating a diverse candidate pool, using behavioral-based interview questions, conducting skills assessments, conducting reference checks, and providing a positive candidate experience. An effective hiring process can help to attract the right candidates, build a strong company culture, and achieve sustainable growth.

Retaining top performers and reducing turnover

Retaining top performers is crucial to the success of a scaling organization. High turnover can be costly and disruptive, and losing top talent can slow down the organization's growth. Here are some strategies for retaining top performers and reducing turnover:

- Provide opportunities for growth and development: Top performers want to work for an organization that values their growth and development. Provide opportunities for learning and development, including mentorship programs, training opportunities, and career advancement opportunities.

- Offer competitive compensation and benefits: Competitive compensation and benefits are important for attracting and retaining top talent. Ensure that your organization is offering competitive salaries, benefits packages, and other incentives.
- Provide a positive work environment: A positive work environment can improve employee engagement and productivity, and reduce turnover. Focus on creating a supportive and inclusive work environment, with opportunities for employees to connect with each other and build relationships.
- Recognize and reward performance: Recognize and reward top performers for their contributions to the organization. This can include bonuses, promotions, and public recognition.

- Provide regular feedback and coaching: Regular feedback and coaching can help to improve employee performance and engagement. Develop a system for providing feedback and coaching to employees on a regular basis.
- Address performance issues promptly: Address performance issues promptly and provide employees with the support they need to improve. This can include additional training, coaching, or counseling.

In summary, retaining top performers requires providing opportunities for growth and development, offering competitive compensation and benefits, creating a positive work environment, recognizing and rewarding performance, providing regular feedback and coaching, and addressing performance issues promptly. These strategies can help to improve employee engagement and productivity, reduce turnover, and achieve sustainable growth.

Chapter 2: Developing Leadership and Management Skills

The qualities of effective leaders in a scaling organization

Effective leadership is critical to the success of a scaling organization. As an organization grows, effective leaders must be able to inspire and motivate their teams, make tough decisions, and adapt to change. Here are some qualities of effective leaders in a scaling organization:

- Visionary: Effective leaders in a scaling organization must have a clear vision of the future and communicate that vision to their team. They should be able to encourage and empower their group to work together toward a shared objective.

- Strategic Thinker: Leaders must be able to think strategically and make tough decisions. They should be able to evaluate options and make decisions based on the long-term goals of the organization.
- Adaptable: As an organization grows, it will face new challenges and opportunities. Effective leaders must be able to adapt to change and make necessary adjustments to keep the organization moving forward.
- Empathetic: Leaders must be empathetic and able to understand the needs and concerns of their team. They should be able to provide support and guidance to their team members when needed.
- Strong Communicator: Effective leaders must be strong communicators, both verbally and in writing. They should be able to clearly and concisely communicate their ideas and vision to their team, stakeholders, and customers.
- Collaborative: Leaders must be able to collaborate with others, both within and

outside the organization. They should be able to build strong relationships and work effectively with others to achieve common goals.

- Results-oriented: Leaders must be results-oriented and focused on achieving the goals of the organization. They should be able to set clear objectives, measure progress, and make adjustments as needed to achieve the desired results.

In summary, effective leaders in a scaling organization must be visionary, strategic thinkers, adaptable, empathetic, strong communicators, collaborative, and results-oriented. These qualities can help leaders to inspire and motivate their teams, make tough decisions, and achieve sustainable growth.

Developing management skills for scaling

As an organization scales, the demands on management increase. Effective managers must be able to lead their teams through change, set clear objectives, and provide guidance and support. Here are some strategies for developing management skills for scaling:

- Invest in management development: Invest in the development of your management team. Provide opportunities for training and development, such as leadership workshops or coaching.
- Provide regular feedback and coaching: Provide regular feedback and coaching to your management team. This can help them to improve their skills and performance, and also help to create a culture of continuous learning.
- Foster a culture of collaboration: Foster a culture of collaboration and teamwork. Encourage managers to work together and share their knowledge and expertise.
- Develop a leadership pipeline: Develop a leadership pipeline by identifying and grooming potential leaders within the organization. This can help to ensure that there is a pool of qualified candidates for leadership roles as the organization grows.

- Encourage innovation: Encourage innovation and creativity among your management team. Provide opportunities for them to try new approaches and experiment with different ideas.
- Set clear objectives and measure progress: Set clear objectives for your management team and regularly measure progress towards those objectives. By doing this, it will be possible to make sure that everyone is working toward the same objectives and forward movement.
- Foster a culture of accountability: Foster a culture of accountability by setting clear expectations for your management team and holding them accountable for their performance. This may contribute to the development of an accountable society.

In summary, developing management skills for scaling requires investing in management development, providing regular feedback and coaching, fostering a culture of collaboration, developing a leadership pipeline, encouraging innovation, setting clear objectives and measuring progress, and fostering a culture of accountability. These strategies can help to ensure that your management team has the skills and abilities to lead the organization through change and achieve sustainable growth

Encouraging continuous learning and development among employees

Encouraging continuous learning and development among employees is critical for the success of a scaling organization. As the organization grows, employees must be able to adapt to change, learn new skills, and take on new responsibilities. Here are some strategies for encouraging continuous learning and development among employees:

- Provide opportunities for training and development: Provide opportunities for employees to participate in training and development programs. This can include workshops, seminars, online courses, or on-the-job training.

- Encourage self-directed learning: Encourage employees to take ownership of their own learning and development. Provide resources such as books, articles, and online courses, and encourage employees to seek out their own learning opportunities.
- Foster a culture of learning: Foster a culture of learning by emphasizing the importance of continuous learning and development. Encourage employees to share their knowledge and expertise with others, and recognize and reward employees who demonstrate a commitment to learning.
- Provide growth opportunities: Provide opportunities for employees to take on new responsibilities and challenges. This can include stretch assignments, cross-functional projects, or leadership development programs.

- Offer mentorship and coaching: Offer mentorship and coaching programs to employees. Pair them with experienced mentors or coaches who can provide guidance and support as they develop their skills and expertise.

- Provide feedback and recognition: Provide regular feedback to employees about their performance and progress, and recognize and reward employees who demonstrate a commitment to learning and development.
- Use technology to support learning: Use technology to support learning, such as online courses, learning management systems, or mobile apps that enable employees to access learning resources anytime, anywhere.

In summary, encouraging continuous learning and development among employees requires providing opportunities for training and development, encouraging self-directed learning, fostering a culture of learning, providing growth opportunities, offering mentorship and coaching, providing feedback and recognition, and using technology to support learning. These strategies can help to ensure that employees have the skills and knowledge they need to succeed in a scaling organization.

Chapter 3: Communication and Collaboration in a Scaling Organization

Building effective communication channels

Effective communication is essential for the success of a scaling organization. As the organization grows, communication becomes more complex, and it is important to establish effective communication channels that ensure that information is shared accurately and efficiently. Here are some strategies for building effective communication channels:

- Establish clear communication protocols: Establish clear communication protocols that outline how information will be shared and who is responsible for sharing it. This can include protocols for meetings, emails, instant messaging, or other communication channels.

- Use technology to support communication: Use technology to support communication, such as video conferencing, collaboration software, or project management tools. This can help to facilitate communication among team members who are working remotely or in different locations.
- Foster open communication: Foster open communication by encouraging team members to share their thoughts and ideas. Create a safe space where team members feel comfortable sharing their opinions, even if they differ from the majority.
- Provide regular updates: Provide regular updates on the progress of projects or initiatives. This can help to keep team members informed and ensure that everyone is working towards the same goals.

- Establish communication channels for feedback: Establish communication channels for feedback, such as surveys, suggestion boxes, or one-on-one meetings. This can help to ensure that team members feel heard and their concerns are addressed.
- Use visual aids: Use visual aids such as charts, graphs, or infographics to convey complex information in a clear and concise manner.
- Encourage face-to-face communication: Encourage face-to-face communication whenever possible, as this can help to build trust and strengthen relationships among team members.

In summary, building effective communication channels requires establishing clear communication protocols, using technology to support communication, fostering open communication, providing regular updates, establishing communication channels for feedback, using visual aids, and encouraging face-to-face communication. These strategies can help to ensure that information is shared accurately and efficiently, and that team members feel connected and engaged with the organization.

Encouraging collaboration across teams and departments

Encouraging collaboration across teams and departments is essential for the success of a scaling organization. As the organization grows, it becomes more complex, and it is important to break down silos and encourage collaboration among different teams and departments. Here are some strategies for encouraging collaboration across teams and departments:

- Foster a culture of collaboration: Foster a culture of collaboration by emphasizing the importance of working together towards common goals. Encourage team members to share their knowledge and expertise with others and recognize and reward collaborative behaviors.

- Establish cross-functional teams: Establish cross-functional teams to tackle complex problems or projects. This can help to break down silos and encourage collaboration among team members who may not typically work together.
- Create opportunities for team-building: Create opportunities for team-building activities that encourage collaboration and communication among team members. This can include team-building exercises, off-site retreats, or social events.
- Use collaboration tools: Use collaboration tools such as project management software, communication tools, or file-sharing platforms. This can help to facilitate collaboration among team members who are working remotely or in different locations.
- Encourage communication across teams and departments: Encourage communication across teams and departments by establishing regular

check-ins, cross-functional meetings, or other communication channels.

- Provide training and development: Provide training and development opportunities that focus on collaboration, communication, and teamwork. This can help team members to develop the skills they need to work effectively with others.
- Recognize and reward collaboration: Recognize and reward collaborative behaviors and achievements. This can help to reinforce the importance of collaboration and encourage team members to continue working together.

In summary, encouraging collaboration across teams and departments requires fostering a culture of collaboration, establishing cross-functional teams, creating opportunities for team-building, using collaboration tools, encouraging communication across teams and departments, providing training and development, and recognizing and rewarding collaboration. These strategies can help to break down silos, build trust and relationships among team members, and ensure that the organization is working towards common goals.

Addressing conflicts and issues in a scaling organization

Addressing conflicts and issues is an essential aspect of managing a scaling organization. As the organization grows, conflicts and issues can become more complex and challenging to resolve. Here are some strategies for addressing conflicts and issues in a scaling organization:

- Identify the root cause of the conflict or issue: Identify the root cause of the conflict or issue by gathering information and talking to all parties involved. Understanding the underlying issues can help to develop effective solutions.
- Encourage open and honest communication: Encourage open and honest communication among team members. Create a safe space where team members feel comfortable sharing their thoughts and ideas.

- Develop a plan for resolution: Develop a plan for resolution that addresses the root cause of the conflict or issue. Involve all parties in developing the plan to ensure that everyone is committed to the solution.
- Mediate the conflict: Mediate the conflict by facilitating a discussion among all parties involved. A neutral third party can help to facilitate the discussion and ensure that all perspectives are heard.
- Implement a conflict resolution process: Implement a conflict resolution process that outlines the steps to follow when conflicts arise. This can help to ensure that conflicts are addressed quickly and effectively.
- Provide training on conflict resolution: Provide training on conflict resolution for all team members. This can help to develop the skills needed to manage conflicts and prevent them from escalating.
- Follow up on the resolution: Follow up on the resolution to ensure that the conflict

has been fully resolved. This can help to prevent the conflict from resurfacing in the future.

In summary, addressing conflicts and issues in a scaling organization requires identifying the root cause of the conflict or issue, encouraging open and honest communication, developing a plan for resolution, mediating the conflict, implementing a conflict resolution process, providing training on conflict resolution, and following up on the resolution. These strategies can help to ensure that conflicts are managed effectively, and the organization can continue to grow and succeed.

Chapter 4: Scaling Operations and Infrastructure

Developing systems and processes that can scale

Developing systems and processes that can scale is essential for managing a growing organization. As the organization grows, it becomes more complex, and it is important to have systems and processes in place to ensure that operations are efficient and effective. Here are some strategies for developing systems and processes that can scale:

- Start with a solid foundation: Start with a solid foundation by defining the organization's mission, values, and goals. This will provide a framework for developing systems and processes that support the organization's objectives.

- Document current processes: Document current processes to identify areas for improvement. This can help to identify inefficiencies and bottlenecks that need to be addressed.
- Standardize processes: Standardize processes to ensure consistency and efficiency. This can include creating standard operating procedures (SOPs) that outline the steps for completing specific tasks.
- Automate processes: Automate processes to reduce manual work and increase efficiency. This can include using software to automate repetitive tasks, such as data entry or reporting.
- Use technology to support scaling: Use technology to support scaling by implementing systems that can handle increased volumes of data or transactions. This can include using cloud-based systems that can scale up or down as needed.

- Develop metrics and key performance indicators (KPIs): Develop metrics and KPIs to measure the effectiveness of processes and systems. This makes it easier to spot problem regions and monitor development over time.
- Continuously improve processes: Continuously improve processes by regularly reviewing and updating SOPs, automating additional tasks, and implementing new technologies as needed.

In summary, developing systems and processes that can scale requires starting with a solid foundation, documenting current processes, standardizing processes, automating processes, using technology to support scaling, developing metrics and KPIs, and continuously improving processes. These strategies can help to ensure that operations are efficient and effective, even as the organization grows and evolves.

The importance of automation in scaling operations

Automation is essential in scaling operations as it allows organizations to increase efficiency, reduce costs, and improve accuracy. Here are some ways in which automation can help to support scaling operations:

- Increased efficiency: Automation can help to increase efficiency by reducing manual work and streamlining processes. This can save time and resources, allowing organizations to handle increased volumes of work without needing to hire additional staff.

- Cost savings: Automation can help to reduce costs by reducing the need for manual labor and minimizing errors. This can help to improve profit margins, making it easier for organizations to scale.

- Improved accuracy: Automation can help to improve accuracy by reducing the likelihood of errors caused by manual work. This can help to ensure that processes are completed correctly and minimize the risk of errors that could lead to customer dissatisfaction or compliance issues.
- Scalability: Automation can be easily scaled up or down to handle increased volumes of work. This allows organizations to handle increased demand without needing to make significant changes to their processes or infrastructure.
- Improved data analysis: Automation can help to improve data analysis by automatically collecting and organizing data. This can provide organizations with insights into their operations, allowing them to identify areas for improvement and make data-driven decisions.

- Improved customer experience: Automation can help to improve the customer experience by reducing wait times and minimizing errors. This can help to increase customer satisfaction and loyalty, supporting continued growth and success.

In summary, automation is essential in scaling operations as it can increase efficiency, reduce costs, improve accuracy, support scalability, improve data analysis, and enhance the customer experience. By implementing automation strategies, organizations can better manage increased volumes of work and position themselves for continued growth and success.

Optimizing infrastructure for growth

Optimizing infrastructure for growth is an important consideration for organizations looking to scale. Here are some strategies for optimizing infrastructure to support growth:

- Scalable infrastructure: Organizations need to invest in infrastructure that can scale as the business grows. This includes scalable IT infrastructure such as cloud-based systems that can be easily scaled up or down depending on the organization's needs.

- Robust security: As an organization grows, so does the risk of cyber-attacks and data breaches. It is important to implement robust security measures to protect sensitive data and prevent security breaches that could damage the organization's reputation.

- Backup and recovery: Implementing backup and recovery systems is essential to ensure that critical data can be restored in case of a disaster or system failure. This can help to minimize downtime and reduce the impact on the business.

- Efficient data management: As an organization grows, the volume of data it generates increases. It is essential to invest in efficient data management systems to ensure that data can be stored, accessed, and analyzed in a timely and effective manner.

- Network infrastructure: Organizations need to invest in robust network infrastructure to support communication and collaboration between employees, customers, and partners. This includes high-speed internet connectivity, virtual private networks (VPNs), and collaboration tools such as video conferencing and instant messaging.
- Capacity planning: Capacity planning involves predicting future growth and ensuring that infrastructure can support that growth. It is important to regularly review and update capacity planning strategies to ensure that infrastructure is prepared to handle future demand.

In summary, optimizing infrastructure for growth involves investing in scalable infrastructure, implementing robust security measures, implementing backup and recovery systems, investing in efficient data management systems, investing in robust network infrastructure, and regularly reviewing and updating capacity planning strategies. By implementing these strategies, organizations can position themselves for continued growth and success.

Chapter 5: Scaling Culture and Values

Maintaining a strong company culture through growth

Maintaining a strong company culture through growth can be a challenge, but it is essential to ensure that the organization remains aligned with its values and mission. Here are some strategies for maintaining a strong company culture through growth:

- Communicate values: It is important to clearly communicate the company's values to new employees and ensure that they are understood and embraced. This can be achieved through regular communication and training programs.

- Encourage transparency: Transparency is essential for building trust and fostering a positive work environment. Encourage transparency by sharing company updates, successes, and challenges with employees and seeking their feedback.
- Foster collaboration: Collaboration can help to build a sense of community and foster a positive work environment. Encourage collaboration by implementing cross-functional teams and promoting teamwork across departments.
- Celebrate success: Celebrating success can help to boost morale and reinforce the company's values. Celebrate successes through company-wide announcements, recognition programs, and team outings.
- Provide development opportunities: Providing development opportunities can help to keep employees engaged and motivated. Offer training programs, mentorship opportunities, and career development plans to help employees grow and advance within the organization.

- Lead by example: Leadership plays a critical role in maintaining a strong company culture. Leaders should embody the company's values and mission and set an example for employees to follow.

In summary, maintaining a strong company culture through growth requires clear communication of values, transparency, collaboration, celebration of success, development opportunities for employees, and leadership by example. By prioritizing company culture and investing in strategies to maintain it, organizations can build a positive work environment that supports continued growth and success.

Ensuring company values are upheld during scaling

Ensuring company values are upheld during scaling is crucial for maintaining the organization's identity and culture. Here are some strategies for ensuring that company values are upheld during scaling:

- Clearly define values: It is important to clearly define the company's values, and ensure that they are communicated effectively to all employees. This includes new hires, existing employees, and leadership.

- Hire for cultural fit: When hiring new employees, prioritize cultural fit alongside skills and experience. Look for candidates who share the organization's values and will be a good fit for the company culture.

- Embed values in processes and policies: Embedding values in processes and policies can help to ensure that they are consistently upheld. For example, if teamwork is a core value, implement collaborative processes and policies to reinforce this value.

- Regularly communicate values: Regularly communicate the company's values through various channels such as company meetings, training sessions, and internal communication channels. This can help to reinforce the importance of the values and ensure that employees are aware of them.

- Lead by example: Leaders play a crucial role in upholding company values. Leaders should embody the values and lead by example, demonstrating the behavior that is expected of all employees.
- Regularly assess values alignment: Regularly assess how well the organization and its employees align with the company's values. This can be done through surveys, feedback sessions, and performance reviews.

In summary, ensuring company values are upheld during scaling requires clearly defining values, hiring for cultural fit, embedding values in processes and policies, regularly communicating values, leading by example, and regularly assessing values alignment. By prioritizing values and investing in strategies to uphold them, organizations can maintain their identity and culture as they grow and scale.

Developing a scalable framework for decision-making and problem-solving

Developing a scalable framework for decision-making and problem-solving is essential for managing growth and ensuring that the organization can make effective decisions in a timely manner. Here are some steps to develop a scalable framework for decision-making and problem-solving:

- Define the problem or decision to be made: Clearly define the problem or decision that needs to be made. This includes identifying the desired outcome and any constraints or factors that need to be considered.
- Gather relevant information: Gather all relevant information, including data, feedback, and input from stakeholders. This may involve conducting research or consulting with subject matter experts.

- Analyze and evaluate options: Analyze and evaluate potential solutions or options, weighing the pros and cons of each. This may involve creating decision matrices or conducting cost-benefit analyses.
- Choose a course of action: Choose the best course of action based on the analysis and evaluation of options. This may involve selecting the option that best aligns with the organization's values and priorities.
- Implement the solution: Once a decision has been made, implement the solution or course of action. This may involve creating an action plan and assigning responsibilities to ensure that the solution is implemented effectively.
- Evaluate the outcome: Evaluate the outcome of the decision or solution to determine its effectiveness. This may involve collecting feedback and data to assess whether the desired outcome was achieved.

- Adjust the framework as needed: Based on the outcome, adjust the decision-making and problem-solving framework as needed to improve future outcomes.

By following these steps, organizations can develop a scalable framework for decision-making and problem-solving that can be applied consistently across departments and teams. This can help to ensure that decisions are made in a timely and effective manner, and that the organization can manage growth while maintaining alignment with its values and priorities.

CONCLUSION

In conclusion, scaling an organization requires effective management strategies that prioritize people, processes, and culture. Developing a scalable framework for decision-making and problem-solving, building an effective hiring process, retaining top performers, developing effective communication channels, encouraging collaboration, and maintaining a strong company culture are all critical components of scaling successfully. Ensuring that company values are upheld during scaling is also crucial for maintaining the organization's identity and culture. By investing in these strategies, organizations can manage growth effectively, maintain alignment with their values, and achieve sustainable success in the long run.

THE SCALING CODE

Reviewing the strategies and techniques covered The book "Scaling People: Strategies and Techniques for Effective Management and Sustainable Company Growth" covers a range of strategies and techniques that are essential for managing growth and scaling an organization. The book begins by defining scaling and the challenges that organizations face when they try to grow too quickly. It then explores the importance of people in scaling and how building a strong company culture that attracts top talent is key to success.

The book also covers important topics such as developing an effective hiring process, retaining top performers, developing effective communication channels, encouraging collaboration, and addressing conflicts and issues in a scaling organization. It also emphasizes the importance of continuous learning and development among employees and the qualities of effective leaders in a scaling organization.

The book also includes practical guidance on developing a scalable framework for decision-making and problem-solving, building effective systems and processes that can scale, optimizing infrastructure for growth, and maintaining a strong company culture through growth. It also discusses the importance of upholding company values during scaling and developing a scalable framework for decision-making and problem-solving.

Overall, the book provides a comprehensive guide to scaling an organization effectively and sustainably. The strategies and techniques covered in the book are practical, actionable, and grounded in real-world experience. The book is a valuable resource for leaders and managers who are looking to manage growth and scale their organizations while maintaining alignment with their values and priorities.

The importance of continuous improvement in scaling people and companies.

Continuous improvement is a critical component of scaling people and companies. As organizations grow and evolve, they need to continually evaluate and refine their processes, systems, and practices to remain competitive and relevant in their markets.

Continuous improvement involves identifying areas for improvement, developing strategies for addressing them, implementing those strategies, and then measuring the results. By taking a data-driven approach to improvement, organizations can make informed decisions about how to allocate their resources and focus their efforts.

In the context of scaling people and companies, continuous improvement means investing in the ongoing development of employees, refining management practices, and optimizing operations to accommodate growth. This requires a commitment to learning and adaptation, as well as a willingness to take risks and experiment with new approaches.

One of the benefits of continuous improvement is that it can help organizations stay ahead of the curve in terms of industry trends and customer needs. By continually refining their practices and processes, organizations can improve their efficiency, productivity, and overall performance, which can lead to increased customer satisfaction and loyalty.

Another benefit of continuous improvement is that it can help organizations stay agile and responsive in the face of change. As organizations scale, they often encounter new challenges and opportunities, and continuous improvement can help them adapt quickly to these changes and capitalize on new opportunities.

In short, continuous improvement is essential for scaling people and companies effectively and sustainably. By investing in ongoing learning and development, refining management practices, and optimizing operations, organizations can achieve their growth objectives while remaining agile and responsive to change.

www.ingramcontent.com/pod-product-compliance
Lightning Source LLC
Chambersburg PA
CBHW071143220526
45467CB00015B/1790